Spirit & truth

THE WAY TO AUTHENTIC WORSHIP

ISBN 978-1-0877-5216-7
Item 005834393
Dewey Decimal Classification Number: 242
Subject Heading: DEVOTIONAL LITERATURE / BIBLE STUDY AND TEACHING / GOD

Printed in the United States of America

Student Ministry Publishing
Lifeway Resources
One Lifeway Plaza
Nashville, Tennessee 37234

We believe that the Bible has God for its author; salvation for its end; and truth, without any mixture of error, for its matter and that all Scripture is totally true and trustworthy. To review Lifeway's doctrinal guideline, please visit www.lifeway.com/doctrinalguideline.

publishing team

Director, Student Ministry
Ben Trueblood

Manager, Student Ministry Publishing
John Paul Basham

Editorial Team Leader
Karen Daniel

Writer
April-Lyn Caouette

Content Editor
Stephanie Cross

Production Editor
Brooke Hill

Graphic Designer
Shiloh Stufflebeam

Table of Contents

Intro

What do you long for most right now? What's the thing you can't stop thinking about? Maybe It's a car or the newest phone. It might be getting accepted into the college of your choice or making a varsity sports team or becoming first chair in the chorus or band. Having goals and dreams is a great thing—it gives us motivation to try our best and strive toward the future. But there's a danger here too: that thing can become more important to us than God. We can find ourselves worshiping it.

Pastor and author Louie Giglio put it this way: "Worship is our response to what we value most . . . [W]orship is all about saying, 'This person, this thing, this experience (this whatever) is what matters most to me . . . it's the thing I put first in my life.'"[1] The Bible says we should worship God alone (Ex. 20:3-5; 34:14; 2 Kings 17:35-36), and as followers of Jesus, that means putting all these other things in their proper place. They cannot be the center of our lives—only God is worthy of that honor.

What exactly does it mean to worship? When we hear the word, we likely think of singing. After all, many of our churches use the phrase "worship team" to refer to the musicians who lead us in song on Sunday mornings. But worship is so much more than that. True worship is an attitude of the heart; it's the way we live our lives for Him above all else. Specific acts of worship are only truly worship if our intent is to honor God.

Over the next thirty days we will look at worship in several different ways. First we'll take a look at some of the ways Jesus worshiped and how people worshiped Him. Then we'll examine what it looks like to worship in Spirit and truth. Additionally, each day's "display" section will give you a practical way that you can explore worship in your own life. We'll learn how to incorporate worship into every area of our lives and put God at the center of everything we do.

Getting Started

This devotional contains thirty days of content, broken down into sections. Each day is divided into three elements—discover, delight, and display—to help you grow in your faith.

discover |

This section helps you examine the passage in light of who God is and determine what it says about your identity in relationship to Him. Included here is the daily Scripture reading and key verses, along with illustrations and commentary to guide you as you learn more about God's Word.

delight |

In this section, you'll be challenged by questions and activities that help you see how God is alive and active in every detail of His Word and your life.

display |

Here's where you take action. Display calls you to apply what you've learned through each day's study.

> **Each day also includes a prayer activity at the conclusion of the devotion.**

Throughout the devotional, you'll also find extra items to help you connect with the topic personally, such as Scripture memory verses and interactive articles that help you go deeper into God's Word.

Spirit and Truth

WHAT IS WORSHIP?

SECTION 1

Worship is an attitude of our hearts toward whatever is most important in our lives. As Jesus followers, the only proper object for our worship is God. As D. A. Carson put it, "worship is the proper response of all moral, sentient beings to God, ascribing all honor and worth to their Creator-God precisely because he is worthy."[2]

The Word Made Flesh

discover

READ JOHN 1:1-18.

The Word became flesh and dwelt among us. We observed his glory, the glory as the one and only Son from the Father, full of grace and truth.

—John 1:14

Everything in the universe was created by God—the heavens and earth, the day and night, the water and land, the plants, the animals, and finally, human beings. Everything exists because He willed it into being. If this wasn't incredible enough, He created it all from absolutely nothing!

That's a bit hard to wrap our heads around. After all, when human beings create, we have to use materials that already exist and change them into new things. When we create a work of art, we take pigments and a canvas and transform them into a painting. When we create a building, we make it out of wood, stone, nails, and plaster. But all these materials were originally created by God!

Jesus—God the Son—was there at the very beginning of time and creation. And He wasn't just there as some kind of divine moral support—John tells us that God created the world through Jesus. Then, at the right time, He became human and lived among us to give us a physical representation of the God of the Universe. We don't need to wonder what God is like because we have seen Him in the flesh. Worshiping Jesus means recognizing Him as fully God, worthy of all our awe, praise, and honor.

delight

What did John mean when he called Jesus "the Word" of God and the "true light that gives light to everyone"? What does this tell us about Jesus?

John meant that Jesus was and is the relatable (to humans) representation of God, and that Jesus was and is the plan to save us from our sin. God has known everything and has had it all planned out forever. Jesus is the "true light" that gives light to everyone because He shows us the way towards God — that way is Jesus Himself. We can come to the Father through Him only, through believing in His sacrifice and Resurrection. The Holy Spirit will then come into us, and we are reborn. This tells us that Jesus loves us and cares about us so much that He came to earth, giving up His rights to reside in heaven, healed us, taught us, and died for us. He is God. He is unfathomably, infinitely loving and merciful. He is the "Way maker," "Peacekeeper," and "Light in the Darkness." He is the display of God's glory.

How can being creative (through things like writing, painting, crafts, dance, or singing) help you grow closer to God and learn about Him?

Being creative can help us express our feelings and thoughts towards God. We can express our deepest concerns, process Scripture, and feel the Holy Spirit teaching us (guiding us in the right direction, too) and renewing our insides. We become more open and closer with God the more we express our deepest thoughts, feelings, and concerns and desires to Him.

display

One way we can be drawn to worship is by spending time in God's magnificent creation. The vastness of the ocean, the grandeur of mountain peaks, the solemn dignity of a forest—these can all fill us with feelings of reverence. Some of the greatest works of art and music have been inspired by the beauty and majesty of the natural world.

Even if you live in the middle of a city, you still can experience wonder at God's creation. Take time to observe details in the world around you. Watch an insect crawling along a blade of grass, or notice all the varieties of color the next time you bite into an apple. Each of these details was put into place by our amazing Creator God.

Take a moment to observe the world around you and reflect on how God's handiwork is present in even the smallest details. Thank God for the good world He created and that He sent us Jesus as a living display of His glory so we could know Him more fully.

To Know Him More

discover

READ LUKE 2:8-20.

Suddenly there was a multitude of the heavenly host with the angel, praising God and saying: Glory to God in the highest heaven, and peace on earth to people he favors!
—Luke 2:13-14

There's so much we don't fully understand about God, yet we're called to give Him praise and honor. We can't look directly in His face, yet He calls us to follow His ways and sing to Him. We might be tempted to think worship is something we do simply because God is so mysterious and seems so distant from us. But then we read that angels worship Him too! If even the angels who live in heaven with Him worship Him, then there must be something more going on.

After the angels announced Jesus's birth to the shepherds, they went to go see the newborn King for themselves. Once they had seen Him and given Him praise, they returned to their lives and shared the news of what they had seen. This sharing was just as much worship as the words of praise and amazement they must have expressed when they saw Him with their own eyes.

Worship is much more than what we say to God—it also includes how we share God with others. We worship not just because He tells us to but because we want to know Him more—and because we want others to know Him more as well.

delight

What are some ways worship helps you grow in your knowledge of who God is?

It helps us process and reflect on all that He has done for us and all that He is. We can worship by witnessing, and in doing that, we'll learn more about others' views and recognize our views.

in youth groups too

What are some ways you can worship that tell other people about God, beyond simply talking about your faith?

I can image Jesus, show His love, and let the Holy Spirit transform and renew my insides. People will see the changes in the way I act, talk, have faith, and dress (and the Jesus stickers!)!

display

When was the last time you were so amazed by God that you just couldn't stay quiet? Maybe it was an answer to prayer or a moving worship service. Maybe you heard an incredible Christian song that you just had to share with someone else. Who did you share it with? What did you share with her? Take a few moments to reflect on something you love about God or a piece of worship music you love and share it with a girl you know today.

Like 5 minutes ago when He shifted my mindsets of swim and my time with Him! It was an incredible relief, and He is leading me down the right path. It strengthened my faith to feel His answer so fast. Not only that, but He also showed me how to get to those better mindsets and growth them! He, as well, gave me the same motive change regarding my writing and looks! I can't wait to share all this with my parents and sister!

Pray that you would be so in awe of God in your daily life that you can't help but share about Him with joy, awe, and thankfulness. Ask Him to give you the courage to talk about Him with the people in your life who do not know Him yet.

Saving Your Best

discover

READ MATTHEW 2:1-12.

*Entering the house, they saw the child with Mary his mother, and falling
to their knees, they worshiped him. Then they opened their treasures
and presented him with gifts: gold, frankincense, and myrrh.*
—Matthew 2:11

How often do we give God our best? If we're honest, we often do the exact
opposite and give Him our least. Often we only pray when we remember
to, or it's a half-hearted prayer just to mark a box in a checklist of things we
know we're supposed to do. When we follow His commands, we often do it
begrudgingly, not truly wanting to but knowing that it's the "right" thing. We
fire off a social media post with a Bible verse then move on with our day.

True worship looks different. When the wise men first saw the star that
signaled the birth of Jesus, they likely traveled hundreds of miles and took
several months for their journey, just to get a glimpse of the newborn King.
They brought precious, valuable gifts with them—gifts that were truly worthy
of a king. Visiting Jesus wasn't just something they did on their way to
somewhere else. Their journey was intentional and full of sacrifice.

If we truly believe God is who He says He is, we will gladly and joyfully give
Him the best of our time, our obedience, our talents, and our attention.
When we give like this, it is an act of worship and service. We set aside time,
energy, and resources because we know His ways are better than anything
we might want outside of Him.

delight

What would it look like for you to give God your best in worship? How might you need to change the way you think about Him for this to become a priority?

I think that it would look like me taking the time to thoughtfully pray and witness, not overthinking or getting distracted by the world, but focusing on God. I need to change the way I see God in my mind for this to become a priority. I have been seeing Him as just some otherworldly being, and not the all-powerful Creator of the universe and Savior of all.

What are the distractions that keep you from worshiping God with your prayers, service, or obedience? How can you put Him above these things?

Distractions include my Christmas gifts, phone, appearance, and the way others view me (and time and no motivation/laziness). To put Him above these things, I need to remember that He is the Creator and Savior and remember His love, patience, and forgiveness, and peace. However, I shouldn't worship Him out of feeling like I owe Him, but out of gratitude and love and the Holy Spirit moving me.

display

Giving God our best in worship means worship is a priority for us, not just an afterthought. It's not something we do just to update our checklists, and it's not something we do just when we think we have time. Find a regular time each day this week to spend worshiping God in a way that works for you. This might be singing a favorite worship song as you get ready for your day or praising Him in prayer for the day that just passed before you turn out the lights to sleep. Regardless of how you worship, make sure it's genuine and the best you have to offer God.

- 8 P.M.

- *Bible plan*
- *Worship*
- *Anxiety Book*
- *Anxiety Devotional*
- *Prayer Journal*

Go to bed at a decent time!

- Morning (Gills till for school)
- Devotional

Find a place where you can spend some uninterrupted moments with God. Set aside the cares of the day for the time being and focus on all the ways He is King over your life. Thank Him for being a King who is worthy of our very best.

DAY 4

Father's House

discover

READ LUKE 2:41-50.

"Why were you searching for me?" he asked them. "Didn't you know
that it was necessary for me to be in my Father's house?"
—Luke 2:49

Only one human in all of history has been able to live a completely
sinless life—Jesus. This is because Jesus was and is both fully God and
fully human. He wasn't God pretending to be a human, and He wasn't
just a human with a special connection to God like the prophets before
Him. Confusing, right? It's a mystery that we won't fully understand until
we are reunited with Him. What we do know is that the relationship
between God the Son (Jesus) and God the Father is unique.

In today's verses, Jesus had traveled to Jerusalem for the annual
Passover festival with His family. When the festival was over, Jesus's
parents headed home, not realizing He had stayed behind. When they
realized He was missing, they hurried back to find Him. He wasn't lost
at all! He was in the temple, learning from the teachers there.

As a boy, Jesus knew the most important things for Him to do were to
study Scripture, learn from teachers, and spend time in the presence
of His heavenly Father. His example shows us what it looks like to
completely devote your life to worshiping God by learning His ways
and serving Him. Like Jesus, we should be learning from people who
are more mature in their faith and aligning our desires with God's by
learning what He loves.

delight

What does it mean for us today to be in our "Father's house"? What or where is this?

This usually means church or a place of worship. This can also mean just spending time with God anywhere (esp. praying & reading His Word).

What are the ways you spend time with your Father and learn about Him throughout your week?

I can do this by praying, doing my devotionals, and reading His Word.

Use resources in the back

Who has God put in your life that you trust to teach you more about God and how to study the Bible?

God has put Chelsea, Gemma, Ben, Aly, Mom, Dad, Ella, and Flaelron's Jim, staff, worship team parents, other in my life that I trust to teach me more about God and how to study the Bible.

display

As Christians today, we tend to think of "worship" and "teaching" as two separate things. But learning about God from a teacher or pastor can be an act of worship in itself if we are listening with a heart desiring to understand more about Him. Think back to the last sermon or teaching you listened to. Were you truly present and listening or were you spacing out? Pray that God would help you to listen to your teachers and pastors this week with curiosity and a desire to truly know and worship God.

Think of a godly woman in your church who has taught you more about God and helped you grow your faith. Take a few minutes and put your creative skills to use to write (and maybe illustrate) a note for her, telling her how much her influence has meant to you.

Chelsea,

Thank you for guiding me so much in my faith. Through your pushes for us to go to church, your devotionals that you gave to all of us at Christmas, and your steady example of a godly woman, I have strengthened my faith and trust in Him and His Will. I have also given my life fully over to Him and His purpose. I have matured and grown as a Christian, and have placed Jesus at the center of my life. Thank you for guiding me in this journey.

Jesus loves you,
Lily

Thank God for the wise pastors and teachers He has brought into your life to help you know Him better. Ask Him to guide these men and women in wisdom and truth, and ask Him to help you be truly present and desire to grow in knowledge and understanding.

He Alone Is Worthy

discover

READ MATTHEW 4:1-11.

Then Jesus told him, "Go away, Satan! For it is written:
Worship the Lord your God, and serve only him."
—Matthew 4:10

The world we live in is filled with things that distract us from God. Many of us carry tiny computers in our pockets that alert us instantly the moment someone sends us a new message or text, "likes" one of our social media posts, or starts following us. We have homework to do, sports and musical instruments to practice, and tests to study for. The world tells us that we should get a good job, pursue romantic relationships, travel to far-off places, buy new clothes and makeup, play more video games . . . the list of things that can fill our thoughts is seemingly endless.

None of these things are bad in and of themselves, and many of them are important things to care about. The problem comes when we start to believe they're the most important things. If we're not careful, we could end up believing these things define us more than our relationship with God. We start looking to them to fulfill us and bring us ultimate satisfaction. They become idols. We start to worship them.

Nothing in this world—not even landing your dream job, dating the perfect guy, or getting into your top college—is worthy of your worship. Only our God is worthy of that honor. Anything we try to place above Him will fall short. He alone is worthy.

delight

What does it look like to worship something other than God? How do we know if we're doing this?

Worshiping something other than God looks like devoting your time, energy, and money to the thing, and valuing it above God and your relationship with Him.

We know we're doing this when we find ourselves spending excess time and money with it and making decisions based on how they would impact the idol rather than your relationship with God

List some of the things you might be tempted to make into idols in your life. How is God greater than all of these things?

— Makeup & Products & Appearance — God created me and dictates what I look like in every way

— Clothes — God created my body and He lasts, while clothes don't
Clothes also have no real, lasting benefit

— Worries & Thoughts & Actions — God gives me the strength to overcome all of my bad worries, thoughts, and actions

He died for me!

— Grades & Swim & high can take away
as possible. They have no real, idolization lasting benefit
They bring momentary pleasure, while God brings infinite pleasure

He gives us all gifts and talents that He can take away

He also gives me wisdom to see where and when I go wrong
He knows every thought and is infinitely patient and forgiving

display

Nothing apart from God is worthy of our worship. Take a moment to think about some of the things that are important to you—your hobbies, your dreams for the future, or even people in your life. Are you treating any of these like they are more important than God? Imagine yourself bringing those things to Jesus and placing them at His feet. This doesn't mean we can't care about these things it just means acknowledging that without Him, they are ultimately meaningless. When He is Lord of our lives, surrendering control of the things that are most precious to us is an act of worship. Below, write down one thing you wish to place at the feet of Jesus today.

Swim

Grades

Confess to God that you sometimes act as though the things of this world are more important than Him or act as though those things can save you in ways that only He can. Thank Him for His mercy and compassion and acknowledge that He alone is the God who is worthy of our worship and praise.

DAY 6

Reconnecting

discover |

READ MATTHEW 14:22-30.

After dismissing the crowds, he went up on the mountain by
himself to pray. Well into the night, he was there alone.
—Matthew 14:23

We'll spend two days on this passage from Matthew looking at worship
from two different angles. First, we'll look at one of Jesus's own
personal practices of worship: prayer.

Jesus had just fed five thousand people with only two fish and five
loaves of bread (see Matt. 14:15-21). Once the leftovers were cleaned
up, Jesus sent His disciples ahead so He could get some alone time. We
might think, "Of course Jesus wanted some alone time! He just
hosted an impromptu dinner party for five thousand people! He must
be exhausted!" But Jesus didn't go away to take a nap. No, Jesus went
into the mountains alone to pray. Not just for ten minutes, either; Jesus
was there "well into the night."

For Jesus, taking time to reconnect with His Father was an important
part of His ministry. He knew that for His mission to succeed, He
needed to be constantly talking to the One whose will He had come to
earth to do (see John 6:38). As children of that same God, we should
follow Jesus's example and make time to spend with God, talking to
Him in prayer and listening to what He says in return. When we do, we
can trust that He will guide our steps (see Prov. 3:5-6) and give us rest
(see Ps. 23:1-4; Matt. 11:28-30; Phil. 4:6-7).

delight

Why do you think it was important for Jesus to spend time alone praying? Why did He still need to pray even though He is God the Son?

It was important for Jesus to spend time alone praying so that He could feel connected to the Father and know what His Will was. He could express it all (His fears about His death) and He would be reassured about His Will. He still needed to pray to know what the Father needed from Him.

Do you have a regular time to pray alone each day? If so, why is this important to you? If not, how can you make this a part of your daily life?

I don't really (excluding my prayer journal). I tend to pray chaotically. I think that sitting down and praying would be better. I can make this a part of my life by setting a time in my head and maybe on my Bible app.

Time: 6:15 A.M. (school mornings)
When I wake up, after and before devotional (on weekends)

display

For some people, kneeling or being seated is the best way to pray. For others, praying while walking feels more natural. Have you ever tried prayer walking? Give it a try today. Find a place where you can walk safely and undisturbed. A nature trail or park might be a good option, or just around your neighborhood. If you feel more comfortable, ask a godly girl friend to go with you and do the same. You may want to bring headphones to listen to some favorite spiritual music, or you may want to simply walk in silence. While you walk, talk with God about the beautiful world He created, or pray for the people and places you pass. Ask Him to show you what He wants you to notice.

Thank God that He delights to listen to our prayers 24/7, wherever we are and whatever we're doing. Thank Him that He longs to spend quiet alone time reconnecting with us, sharing His heart and hearing what's on ours—not because He doesn't already know but because He wants to grow closer to us with each passing day.

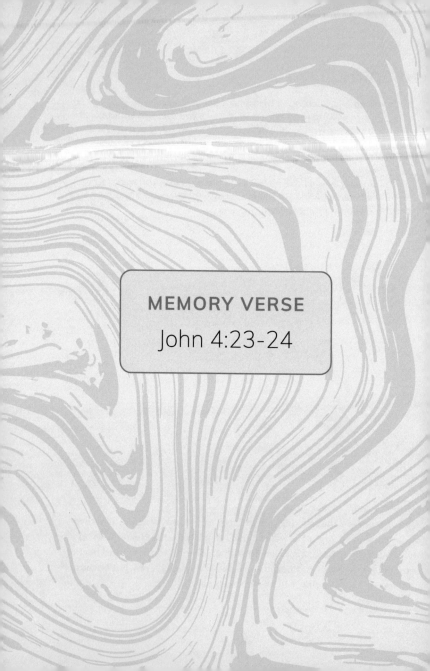

MEMORY VERSE

John 4:23-24

"But an hour is coming, and is now here, when the true worshipers will worship the Father in Spirit and in truth. Yes, the Father wants such people to worship him. God is Spirit, and those who worship him must worship in Spirit and in truth."

Awe and Wonder

discover

READ MATTHEW 14:22-33.

When they got into the boat, the wind ceased. Then those in the boat worshiped him and said, "Truly you are the Son of God."
—*Matthew 14:32-33*

Have you ever seen something so amazing that it left you speechless? Maybe your family took a trip to the Grand Canyon and it was more awesome than you could describe. Or maybe you saw a girl do an unbelievable dance routine or heard a solo that blew you away. When we see something amazing, sometimes we can't find the words to describe it and are just silent in awe for a moment, or we just can't stop talking about how incredible it was.

This is what happened for Jesus's disciples that day in the boat. First they saw Him walking on the water, a sight so unbelievable that they thought He was a ghost. No living human could do that! Then they saw Peter walk on the water at Jesus's command—just for a moment but long enough to stun them. Finally, as He stepped into the boat, the mighty wind stopped suddenly, as if He had commanded it.

The disciples didn't know what else to do. They fell on their faces and praised Jesus as the Son of God. He had just done things they could never have imagined in their wildest dreams. There was no other explanation but that He was God in the flesh. They were filled with awe and wonder.

delight

Think about a time you experienced something so amazing, you didn't know what to say. Describe how that felt. How could you praise God in moments like these?

It felt absolutely incredible when God answered my prayers about my products and my vanity and my handwriting. It felt like such a huge relief, like a balloon inside of me had popped and a huge weight had been taken off of my shoulders. It felt like a light had been flicked on, like a door had opened, and like I'd finally spotted the right path. I can praise God in these moments by being sincere with Him about my thanks, even saying to Him that I'm speechless. I can also praise Him by sharing these experiences with others.

What are some things Jesus has done in your life that left you full of awe and wonder? How has He blessed you or the girls around you in amazing ways?

He has answered my prayers exactly when I was doing and/or thinking about what I'd prayed about. He has timed His answers perfectly and lovingly and mercifully. He has forgiven me of sin while I'm sinning and, hypocritically, praying to Him about it. He's given me and the girls around me (at least I think) a sense of identity in Christ, financial safety (and benefits) and have put us in situations and trials that have strengthened/are strengthening/will strengthen our faith in Him.

Spirit and Truth

display

When we gather as a church to pray and worship together, we are doing what the disciples did—declaring that He is Lord and that He alone is worthy of our praise. We can do this in smaller groups too. Ask a believing girlfriend or family member to spend a few moments in prayer with you today. Pray aloud, praising God for all the ways He amazes you and that His ways are more incredible than anything the world can offer. Spend some time sharing with each other about how God has shown up in your lives lately.

Take some time to praise God today. If it helps, use the words from some of your favorite worship songs to remind you of His amazing attributes: His unfailing love, His justice and mercy, His faithfulness, His unending patience, or His perfect wisdom, just to name a few.

DAY 8

Not Just Singing

discover

READ MATTHEW 26:26-30.

After singing a hymn, they went out to the Mount of Olives.
—Matthew 26:30

Worship in our modern church is so tied to music, and particularly to singing, that it may surprise you to learn that this moment—which appears in both Matthew and Mark's Gospels—is the only recorded instance we have of Jesus singing! This doesn't mean singing is unimportant. The Bible is filled with stories of God's people singing songs of praise, lament, victory, and mourning—we even have an entire book dedicated to songs (the book of Psalms). In the book of Revelation, John tells about the vision he had of multitudes singing praises to the Lord in heaven (see Rev. 5:8-14). Clearly singing is an important part of worship!

Right before they sang this hymn, in a quiet, peaceful moment the night before the horror of His crucifixion, Jesus shared a moment with His disciples in a different kind of worship. In a private upper room, gathered together with only His closest friends, Jesus taught them how to honor Him after He was gone. He taught them to remember Him by breaking bread and drinking the cup as symbols of His sacrifice and all it accomplished. When we participate in this same sharing of bread and cup in what we now call the Lord's Supper, we are participating in a profound act of worship.

Spirit and Truth

delight

Have you ever participated in the Lord's Supper (also known as Communion)? How did the bread and juice remind you of Jesus's sacrifice on the cross?

I have, but only once or twice. It reminded me of Jesus's sacrifice on the cross because I could tie the story of the Lord's Supper to the actions and taste. The story and sacrifice felt (and feels) more tangible and closer to me and understandable.

What did Jesus mean when He said the bread is His body and the cup is His blood?

Jesus meant that, when we break and eat the bread, which represents His broken body, and drink the wine, which represents His spilled blood (which confirms the Lord's covenant), we are worshiping and remembering Him and His sacrifice.

Why is the Lord's Supper something we do together as a church and not just as individuals? What does this teach us about worship?

The Lord's Supper is something we do together as a church because Jesus saved all of us, humankind, from our sins. This makes the importance and powerfulness of His sacrifice so much greater. This teaches us that worship should be done together as we understand and see God's power and Jesus's sacrifice as greater.

display

Different churches celebrate the Lord's Supper in different ways and at different times. Some churches celebrate it every week; others celebrate it once a month or quarter. Next time you observe the Lord's Supper with your church, take an extra moment to reflect on Jesus's death and what His broken body and spilled blood made possible for us believers. Thank Him for this amazing gift of life!

Even if you only celebrate the Lord's Supper occasionally, you can worship Jesus at any mealtime by praying before you eat. Next time you gather together for a meal with your family or other believers, ask if you can pray aloud before you all eat. If you're not sure what to pray, you might start with a simple prayer like the one listed below.

"**Dear heavenly Father: We thank you for this food set before us. Bless the hands that prepared it. May it be a nourishment to our bodies, and use our bodies for Your service. In Jesus's name we pray, amen.**"[3]

Everywhere

discover

READ LUKE 24:50-53.

After worshiping him, they returned to Jerusalem with great joy.
—Luke 24:52

If someone asked you, "Where do you go to worship?", the automatic answer for most of us would be, "My church building." For the ancient Israelites, the answer would have been "the temple." Both answers only cover a small portion of the ways we can worship.

On the day Jesus went back to heaven, He was with His disciples in Bethany, a few miles outside of Jerusalem. He blessed them, and they worshiped Him joyfully. Then they returned to the temple in Jerusalem and continued to praise Him there. As Jews, they had been taught that the temple in Jerusalem was the dwelling place of God and that it was the proper place to worship Him. But when they were with Jesus in person, they worshiped Him wherever He was.

Worship is more than just the things we do—it is the way we live. We should worship Jesus in every moment of every day—in the way we speak, eat, care for one another, and share His name with others. Because the Holy Spirit lives in us, we can worship Him wherever and whenever. We no longer need to seek God only in the temple or a church building because He lives within each and every believer who professes Jesus as Lord. Like the disciples, we can worship God where He is: right here with each of us.

delight

List some of the places and ways you worship God.

Singing

Praying

Devotionals

Reading His Word

Phone Screen

Church

Home

School

TKD

Track

Ways to worship God continually:
- Be polite & an honest role model to others
- Pray to Him as a humble servant not deserving to even speak to Him
- Thank God for the little things
- Give Him your worries

What does it mean to worship God continually? What could this look like in your daily life?

Worshipping God continually means praising Him, spreading the Word, reading Scripture,etc. consistently in our daily lives. I can pray praises throughout the day, e.g. at the beginning and end, and can stay on track and add plans and devotionals I can also tell my story and spread the Good News at home and at school.
ˣ & other places

How can you see worship as more than just what you do but as an attitude of your heart?

Worship is something meaningful that we can live. We can live worship by spreading the faith, reading and memorizing Scripture, etc.

See Him as Sovereign King of everything
Be internally grateful for His love & let your love & gratefulness overflow into worship

display

How would it change your relationship with God if you worshiped every moment of the day? This might seem difficult, but you can practice this kind of continual worship right now. American missionary Frank Laubach wrote a devotional called *The Game with Minutes*, in which he urged believers to spend at least one second of each minute remembering God. "We do not need to forget other things, or stop our work," he wrote, "but we invite Him to share everything we do or say or think."[4] Maybe we can't manage one second out of every minute, but remembering a few of his simple prayers below can help us to worship God throughout our day.

Any moment of the day: "What, Father, do you desire said? What, Father, do you desire done this minute?"[5]

When you're walking alone: "Dear Father, what are you telling me through this, and this, and this?"[6]

When you're studying: "God . . . Help my wavering thoughts to concentrate so that I may not waste a moment. Show me what is worth remembering."[7]

Spirit and Truth

discover

READ JOHN 4:1-26.

"But an hour is coming, and is now here, when the true worshipers will worship the Father in Spirit and in truth. Yes, the Father wants such people to worship him. God is spirit, and those who worship him must worship in Spirit and in truth."
—John 4:23-24

As Jesus was traveling, He encountered a Samaritan woman at a well. Thirsty from His travels, He asked if she would give Him some water. The woman saw He was a Jew and was amazed He would even speak to her. Jesus responded in a rather strange way. He said that if she knew who He was, she would have asked Him for "living water." What did He mean? Jesus wasn't talking about literal water but the nourishment and eternal life that comes from the gospel.

She and many other Samaritans in her town believed in Jesus that day. But for them to truly have access to the "living water" Jesus offered, they needed a right understanding of worship. She wanted to know about the correct place to worship (see v. 20), but Jesus focused on the correct attitude for worship. The "where" wasn't important. What mattered was that the worship was authentic, done "in Spirit and in truth" (v. 24).

The rest of our devotions will look at what this means. We've learned about different forms our worship can take, but they won't mean anything if we don't know the truth of who we're worshiping or the Spirit who allows us to have a relationship with Him.

delight

Why might the woman have wanted to know where the proper place to worship was? Why was this the wrong question to ask?

The woman might have wanted to know which place was correct for worship so that she could worship better. This was the wrong question to ask because she wasn't focused on the worship itself, which is crucial.

When have you gone on "auto-pilot" while worshiping—singing worship songs or praying just because you knew it was what you were "supposed" to do? What did your relationship with God feel like at these times?

I go on auto-pilot when praying from my prayer journal and reading (and praying) prayers. I also go on auto-pilot when apologizing, thanking the Lord, and asking for help. My relationship didn't feel like anything, and certainly not stronger, because I wasn't paying attention to it at these times.

display

When we worship God from a place of Spirit and truth, we are joining together with countless other believers throughout history. As Marianne Meye Thompson points out, "Worship serves the indispensable function of uniting us with 'all the saints,' living and dead . . . [it reminds] us that we worship not merely as a congregation or a church, but as part of the church, the people of God. . . . [W]orship is a participation in the unceasing celestial praise of God."[8]

How does worship connect you to all other believers—past, present, and future?

*Feel I say the same things   Holy Spirit
United as believers*

List the names of some of the women of older generations, girls your own age, and girls younger than you who you worship with because they are also worshiping God, whether you get to worship together physically or not.

*Gamma   Eve   Hazel
Chelsea   Ruby
Mom*

Ask God to fill your heart with gratitude for the many believers who have come before you, worshiping and serving God with their whole hearts and minds. Pray that He would join you together in Spirit with the global body of Christ throughout history and prepare you for the glorious day when we will all worship Him together as "a vast multitude from every nation, tribe, people, and language" (Rev. 7:9).

Spirit and Truth

SPIRIT

SECTION 2

When we worship "in Spirit" (John 4:23), we worship from a genuine place of reverence, awe, love, and gratitude for God. We also worship through the power of the Holy Spirit, who enables us to align our wills and our passions with His.

DAY 11

Born of the Spirit

discover

READ JOHN 3:1-8.

"Whatever is born of the flesh is flesh, and whatever is born of the Spirit is spirit."
—John 3:6

We all want to know the things we need to do to get everything we want in life. After all, that's what our culture teaches us. If you work hard enough and do the right things, good things happen. It's all about putting in the work. Right? Fortunately, the kingdom of God doesn't work this way. We don't enter the kingdom of God by doing the "right" things. God doesn't want us to earn our way into His presence like we'd earn a good grade by studying hard or work to make the team or first chair.

Worshiping God isn't about trying harder to "feel" spiritual feelings. It's about growing in a relationship with Him, and we can only do that through the power of His Holy Spirit living in us and with us. When we acknowledge Jesus as Lord, something starts to happen. We receive the Holy Spirit and He begins to work in us, transforming our hearts and minds so that we grow to be more like Him. We are "born again" by the Spirit. Without the Spirit, the words of Jesus are just words. They can't begin to take root in our lives until we see Him as more than just a teacher and a prophet, but as the Son of God and Lord of our lives.

delight

What are some ways you try to "work harder" at worshiping God or growing your relationship with Him? How can you instead simply be in His presence?

> I try to pray about every wrong thing I do and obsess over every little thing, trying to make my relationship with Him "clean" and "perfect." Instead, I can just bask in His presence throughout the day, not obsessing.

How do you know if you have been "born again"?

You know you've been born again when you start to be pushed to change certain things and when you feel Jesus's Word start to have meaning. There isn't an "Aha!" moment, exactly; just a flicker that grows into a raging fire, if you let it.

Spirit and Truth

display

Choose a short passage of Scripture—one of your favorites, something you're studying, or even today's devotional passage. Read it once, looking for words that stand out to you. Write these words in a journal. Read it again, paying closer attention to the words that stood out to you. What is God trying to teach you through this passage right now? How does it apply to your life? Let the Spirit guide you as you write down your reflections. Read it one more time, asking the Spirit to speak to you through this passage as you go about your day.

> man
> leader
> Rabbi
> miraculous
>   evidence
>   truth
>   see
>   womb
>   assure
>   of water
>   spiritual life
> don't be surprised
>   born of the Spirit

Thank God that we don't need to earn our place in His kingdom and that worship isn't something we need to "do better" by working at it. Thank Him that we grow in our relationship with Him through the work of the Holy Spirit, not our own power, and that as we grow closer to Him, our ability and desire to worship and praise Him grows as well.

DAY 12

Dependent on Him

discover |

READ LUKE 2:25-35.

When the parents brought in the child Jesus . . . Simeon took him up
in his arms, praised God, and said, "Now, Master, you can dismiss
your servant in peace, as you promised. For my eyes have seen your
salvation. You have prepared it in the presence of all peoples."
—Luke 2:27–31

Why did some people—like Simeon—accept Jesus willingly while others opposed Him violently? For Simeon, the key is six words in verse 25: "the Holy Spirit was on him." Because the Holy Spirit was with him, he was filled with praise for the infant Jesus and worshiped Him with whole-hearted love and reverence.

In the Gospel of Luke, Jesus prayed, "I praise you, Father, Lord of heaven and earth, because you have hidden these things from the wise and intelligent and revealed them to infants" (Luke 10:21; see also Matt. 11:25). The "wise and intelligent" people He was talking about were those people who thought they had it all together and didn't need God. The "infants," on the other hand, were people who acknowledged that they couldn't do anything or know anything without the power of God in their lives—they knew they were dependent on Him for everything.

The hardness of heart that prevents people from acknowledging their dependence on God also prevents the Holy Spirit from working in their lives. If we can admit that we need God, then His Spirit can invade our lives and hearts.

delight

What does it look like to be dependent on God? Why is this important for our worship?

Being dependent on God means giving Him everything and following His will in every decision. We trust Him to lead us through life and with our problems, though it is important to remember that God isn't a magic genie who just fixes our problems. This is important because our worship isn't genuine if we aren't depending on God, because we don't trust Him fully.

In our world, independence is seen as a good thing and dependence is seen as weak or immature. How is this different in the kingdom of God?

In the kingdom of God, we are infants, relying on God. That doesn't mean we're not smart enough or strong enough, but that we have come to realize that we need God.

What are some ways you might need to shift your thinking about dependence and independence in your daily life? How might that change the way you worship?

I can pray to God and follow what He tells me (Scripture, etc.) in every decision and situation. I can pray to Him about my worries and stop worrying about them after I pray. My worship will be more genuine, personal, meaningful, and grateful now.

display

Singing hymns can be a beautiful way to worship God and confess our dependence on Him. They might seem old-fashioned to you, especially if you don't attend a church that regularly sings them. But today, look up a few hymns online and try singing along with them. (You can find lyric videos on YouTube if you don't know the words.) You can even find updated versions with modern music. You never know—they may become your new favorite worship songs! Here are a few suggestions:

- "I Need Thee Every Hour" performed by Jars of Clay

- "Turn Your Eyes Upon Jesus" performed by Noah James & the Executives

- "Great is Thy Faithfulness" performed by Austin Stone Worship

- "How Deep the Father's Love for Us" performed by Austin Stone Worship

Think of a few girls who might like to join you in singing hymns. Ask a parent or guardian to help you host a "night of worship" in your house, where you and a few girlfriends can get together, talk about what the Lord has been teaching you lately, and maybe sing a few modern hymns.

> **Ask God to show all the ways you are dependent on Him in life. Ask Him to grow your humility and to forgive you for all the times you believed you didn't need Him. Praise Him for all the ways He sustains you, provides for you, and grows you in His wisdom.**

DAY 13
The Unpopular Choice

discover

READ LUKE 4:16-29.

He came to Nazareth, where he had been brought up. As usual, he
entered the synagogue on the Sabbath day and stood up to read.
—Luke 4:16

As we walk with Christ, we'll often need to choose: Do we do the popular thing or the thing that honors God even though it feels socially risky? Do we follow our friends even into sin? Or do we stand strong in our convictions? Hopefully our friends will accept our decisions, but they might not, especially if they aren't following Christ. They might make fun of us or even lose respect for us.

In Jesus's first recorded sermon, we see Jesus make this choice. He wasn't preaching in some far-off city where no one knew Him. He was in His hometown, surrounded by people who knew Him and recognized Him as Joseph's son (see v. 22). After He finished reading, He could have simply sat down, but the Spirit prompted Him to continue speaking. His listeners went quickly from being pleased with His words (see v. 22) to enraged just a few moments later (see v. 28). They had hoped to see Him perform miracles for them like He had done in Capernaum, but He had a very different, unpopular message to share with them.

Following Jesus and His ways won't always be the popular decision. But we know the Spirit is both our guide and our comforter. He will give us the conviction to do the things that honor God and the courage to make hard choices for the sake of His name.

delight

How have you experienced (or seen your Christian friends experience) the disapproval of others when you made a choice that honored God but wasn't popular? Why did you make that choice?

I haven't really experienced disapproval but I've experienced (z rhime) judgement. I felt pulled by the Holy Spirit and remembered all that Jesus does for me.

What are some difficult, unpopular choices that God might be calling you to make right now? How can the Holy Spirit help you?

God is calling me to make my Converse Christian and to wear them less and not for popularity. God is calling me to spend less time putting On makeup and more time in His Word God is calling me to talk to my friends about my story. The Holy Spirit can guide me, giving me courage, wisdom, strength, and/or peace.

display

Sometimes one of the most difficult things believers can do is share our faith with others—yet it's also the most important. Jesus called us to "make disciples of all nations" (Matt. 28:19) and "preach the gospel to all creation" (Mark 16:15), but often we're afraid of what people will think of us.

Talking about our beliefs proudly and without fear is an act of worship. Pray for opportunities to speak about Him with your friends and family today. It may not feel comfortable at first, but if we are letting the Spirit lead us, sharing our faith can become as natural as sharing any other aspect of our lives.

As you pray, keep an index card handy. Jot down the names of any girls who need to know about God. Keep this card with you as a reminder to pray for them and speak with them about Him when you can.

Thank God that He challenges us to do hard things, like follow Him and speak about Him even when it's unpopular. Ask Him to convict you through the Spirit when you are tempted to take the easy way out of a situation instead of making the choice that most honors Him. Ask Him for the courage to follow Him and talk about Him boldly, no matter the cost.

Hearing but not Accepting

discover |

READ JOHN 6:60-71.

"The Spirit is the one who gives life. The flesh doesn't help at all. The words that I have spoken to you are spirit and are life."
—John 6:63

In the fishing village of Capernaum, a large crowd had gathered because of the miracles Jesus was performing. They could see there was something special about Jesus—they even believed He was the Messiah! However, they had a different idea about what that meant than Jesus did. As they listened to Jesus's words (see vv. 26-59), they became uncomfortable. They had been expecting a prophet who would become the new king of Israel. They had expected someone who would topple the Roman government. They did not expect someone who claimed to be God Himself, and they didn't really know what to make of what He was saying.

"When many of his disciples heard this, they said, 'This teaching is hard. Who can accept it?'" (v. 60). Although the crowd "heard," they could not "accept" what Jesus taught. The Twelve, however, stayed because they believed Jesus's words were truly from God. They knew the best place to be was right by Jesus's side. The crowd was relying on their natural understanding—their "flesh"—to understand Jesus. Jesus can only be understood through the Spirit. Worshiping Jesus in Spirit means that when we hear His words, we also accept them because we know they are Spirit-led (see John 3:34). His words may not always be easy, but we can trust that they are always good and true.

delight

When are you most tempted to ignore Jesus's teachings? When are they most difficult for you to follow?

I am most tempted to ignore Jesus's teachings at school. They are also most difficult to follow at school. Really, I tend to block Jesus and the Holy Spirit out anytime I'm in public, especially with people my own age and my friends.

What are some messages the world gives us that are easier to follow than Jesus's? How can you remember that Jesus is still the only One worth following and worshiping, even when it's hard?

Some messages that the world gives include "Youth doesn't last forever, so experience everything" and "Virginity is lame." I can remember that Jesus is the only one worth following and worshiping when I remember the Crucifixion, the Resurrection, the Holy Spirit, and eternal life.

display

Sometimes we don't want to worship. We might be going through something difficult, and we might not feel particularly grateful to God. Thankfully, God can handle all of our doubts and emotions—even our anger.

Even at times like this, we can worship. Simple prayers are powerful. Today, decide on a simple prayer or two you can use when you're struggling. You could try, "Help me, God!", "God, be near me," or "God, You are good." When you can't find words to pray, a simple prayer like this can remind you that He is still with you.

Take a few deep, calming breaths and take a moment to be present with God. Thank Him for giving you new life and understanding through the Spirit. Ask Him to draw nearer to you when His teachings are hard and to give you strength to persevere in your faith when it feels like it would be easier to give up.

Secret No More

discover

READ LUKE 10:21-24.

Then turning to his disciples he said privately, "Blessed are the eyes that see the things you see!"
—*Luke 10:23*

Do you love learning secrets? Most of us do. There's something special about learning something not many people know. If a girl friend shares one of her secrets with us, it means she trusts us enough to appreciate how precious that secret is and to keep it safe. That kind of trust is a privilege that usually has to be earned.

One of the amazing things about Jesus was that the men He chose as His closest disciples didn't do anything to earn their place by His side. They were there simply because Jesus chose them. He chose them even knowing that one of them would betray His trust! Through the work of the Spirit, they were granted access to understand things about God that no one ever had before—and all because it was the Father's "good pleasure" (v. 21).

We, too, have access to this understanding about God through the work of the Holy Spirit in us. What was once secret has been revealed. Because of the unique relationship between Father, Son, and Spirit, God works and lives in us eternally through His Spirit, growing us and changing us as we serve and worship Him through His Son, Jesus. Each of us receives this incredible gift when we acknowledge Jesus as our Lord, and it's a gift that can never be taken away.

delight

What are some things about God that the Spirit helps you understand or accept?

Some things about God that the Spirit helps me understand are that God is the Beginning and the End and that He is the I Am. The Spirit helps me understand and see the Holy Trinity as 3 bodies, but 1 Person.

What are the aspects of God about which you would like to have more understanding?

These aspects include understanding His infinite mercy, forgiveness, power, and love. I also want to better understand why God created humans and satan.

How can you allow the Spirit to work in you to grow your understanding in these areas?

I can read the Word and listen for the Spirit. I can listen to the Spirit anytime, too.

display

Reading the prayers of Jesus and other believers can help us worship with a different perspective. Look up some of the following prayers in your Bible or online and write down or print a few of your favorites. Post them somewhere you can see them regularly and read them prayerfully whenever you see them. If they stir any thoughts in you, record these in a prayer journal or notebook and refer back to them from time to time.

- The Lord's Prayer (Matt. 6:9-13; Luke 11:2-4)

- A prayer of David for wisdom and forgiveness (Ps. 39:4-13)

- A prayer of Paul for spiritual power (Eph. 3:14-19)

- Jonah's prayer from inside the great fish (Jonah 2:1-9)

- The Peace Prayer of St. Francis

- The Serenity Prayer

Thank God for the incredible gift of the Holy Spirit, who works in us and through us and enables us to understand things that were once hidden. Ask the Spirit to grow your understanding more and more each day as you follow Jesus and worship Him.

DAY 16

Peter's Confession

discover

READ LUKE 5:1-11.

When Simon Peter saw this, he fell at Jesus's knees and said, "Go away from me, because I'm a sinful man, Lord!"
—Luke 5:8

What is the grossest thing you can think of? How do you talk about it? Chances are, you make jokes because that's what humans often do when things are uncomfortable. We turn them into jokes to make them feel less serious.

When it comes to things that are uncomfortable and gross, sin is at the top of the list. None of us like looking at all the ways we fall short, especially when we think they will earn us condemnation. When Peter saw Jesus's power and looked at his own sin in comparison, he didn't know what to do but cry out in dismay. Standing next to the holiness of God, Peter knew he could never measure up.

The good news is that because of Jesus, we've been forgiven of our sin, now and forever. We fear that God won't accept us because we're too sinful—but this just isn't true! God loves us so much that He sent His Son to die for us, even though we couldn't possibly stop being sinful enough to deserve it. He gave Himself so that our sin would be forgiven and our relationship with the Father would be restored.

Of course, we still need to acknowledge our sin. In fact, confessing our sin is how we are able to truly worship. When we can see all the ways we fall short, we can see how truly incredible our God is and how much we need Him. We can turn away from our sin and turn toward Him in love, gratitude, and praise.

delight |

How do you typically define "confession"? How might this be different from the way Luke would have defined it in today's passage?

I think that confession is typically defined as the admittance of a wrong. However, in today's passage, it means turning from our sin after repenting and following Jesus.

How does confessing our sin to God and others prepare us to worship?

Confessing our sin to God and others prepares us to worship because it makes us remember God's forgiveness and sacrifice.

How is confession a form of worship itself?

Confession is a form of worship itself because we are remembering how we'll always fall short and see how much we need Him and how much He loves us. We can turn away from our sin with gratitude.

display

You may think that to confess sin, you need to talk to a pastor or another person of spiritual leadership in your life. It can certainly help to talk to a trusted believer when something is troubling you, but confession is first and foremost between you and God.

Today, take a moment to think about the ways you have not been faithful to God and confess these to Him, trusting that He is faithful not only to forgive but also to help you turn away from your sin and more fully toward Him.

Think about a Christian girl friend you know you can trust. If you don't have an accountability partner, consider asking her to prayerfully commit to having this kind of relationship with you. You can get together to talk with about what you're both learning about God, confess your struggles, encourage each other, and pray together.

If you're not sure what words to say when you are confessing, you can start with the prayer below.

Lord, forgive me. So often I try to do things my own way instead of looking to You for guidance. Even when I know what You are calling me to do, I often do something else that seems better to me at the time. Lead me in Your righteousness and help me to love Your ways. In Jesus's name, amen.

Memory Verse

JOHN 6:63

"The Spirit is the one who gives life. The flesh doesn't help at all. The words that I have spoken to you are spirit and are life."

Dirty Dishes

discover

READ MATTHEW 23:25-28.

*"Woe to you, scribes and Pharisees, hypocrites! You are like whitewashed
tombs, which appear beautiful on the outside, but inside are full
of the bones of the dead and every kind of impurity."*
—*Matthew 23:27*

Imagine if the next time you did the dishes, you only washed the outside of
your family's mugs. On the shelf, they would look spotless. But the next time
you used one, you'd be mixing your drink with last week's coffee or orange
juice—maybe even some mold. What looked great from the outside was
actually pretty gross on the inside.

In contrast to Peter's genuine confession of sinfulness in Luke 5:8, the
Pharisees believed they were doing the right things to worship God. They
were actually more like the mugs in our example: they looked clean—
worshiping in ways that seemed good—but on the inside they were full
of greed and self-centeredness. This hypocrisy—presenting themselves
one way but acting in another—was preventing them from having a true
relationship with Him.

All of us continue to wrestle with sin; this is part of living in a broken world.
So we have a choice: Will we pretend we can fix the problem ourselves, like
the Pharisees? Or will we admit that we need God to change us from the
inside out? This is the heart of genuine worship through the Spirit: First we
acknowledge that without God, we're powerless to fix our sin problem. Then
we praise Him for giving us a way to be made new through Jesus.

delight

Think back to a time in your life when you pretended you were right with God but deep down you knew you weren't. How did that affect your ability to worship Him?

At school, I feel off. I feel disconnected as I try to be with Him throughout my day. This prevents me from genuinely worshiping Him.

What is an area of your life where you have been trying to hide sin rather than admitting you can't fix it on your own?

Clothes & Popularity

I try to hide and sneak in popularity, thinking God doesn't see me. I also often overanalyze everything when I do feel guilty

What are some steps you can take today to confess your sin to God? How can you confess your dependence on Him and let Him work in your heart?

I can pray and let Him change my view. I can worship through my actions and the way I present myself to the world. I can challenge myself to obey the Spirit,

display

One form of worship that can easily become hypocrisy is our giving. Jesus taught that when we give of our money or resources, we shouldn't make a big show of it (see Matt. 6:1-4). Today, brainstorm some ways that you can give to others anonymously. Maybe you can offer to pay for the order of the person behind you in a drive-thru line, give a little extra on your church's online giving app this week, or volunteer to do some behind the scenes work at your church. Put one of these plans into action and pray that God would use your generosity for kingdom purposes.

Take some time to examine your heart and see if there are any areas where you are covering up sin with acts that seem righteous on the outside. Confess this sin to God and ask Him to help you repent (turn away) from attitudes and behaviors that don't please Him. Humbly ask Him to show you how to walk more in line with His ways.

DAY 18

Traditions

discover

"This people honors me with their lips, but their heart is far from me. They worship me in vain, teaching as doctrines human commands."
—Matthew 15:8-9

Have you ever been accused of not being a "real" fan of something? Maybe you didn't know some trivia that someone else thought all "real" fans should know. Maybe you were wearing a band t-shirt and someone accused you of not being a "real" fan because you couldn't list enough of their songs. In today's culture this is called "gatekeeping"—saying certain people can't be part of a community because they don't know or do the "right" things. Gatekeepers want to keep outsiders out and control who the insiders are.

That's what we see the Pharisees doing here. Jesus and His disciples weren't following all the rules the Pharisees thought were necessary for true followers of God, such as ceremonial hand-washing before meals. So they asked Jesus, accusingly, why His disciples were ignoring the tradition. In their eyes, Jesus's disciples were being bad worshipers.

Jesus turned the Pharisees' accusation back on them, pointing out that they were following man-made traditions in a way that contradicted God's commandments. Ironically, the traditions had been created to help apply Scripture, but in the process of following traditions, they had lost sight of following God.

Let's not get caught up in whether we're doing worship the "right way" or not. Traditions aren't necessarily bad, but true worship is anything that comes from a genuine spirit of love for God and a heartfelt desire to honor His Word.

Spirit and Truth

delight

List some of the ways you, your family, or other Christians you know worship or practice spiritual traditions.

- Pray at night
- Go to church esp. on Easter & Christmas
- Try to do extra Christian stuff in December
- Say grace

How do these practices honor God and His commandments?

- Thank God
- Show our affection for Him
- Grow our relationships with Him
- Remind ourselves of what Jesus did
- Feels bad if we don't smtimes

Is there a way to engage in these practices that could dishonor God or contradict His commandments? What might that look like?

- Airplane mode / Autopilot
- Only saying it so we don't feel guilty
- Doing it because it's "right"
- Doing it bc others are doing it

display

Holidays are a common time for us to honor traditions passed down through the generations. Whether it's lighting candles for Advent, searching for eggs at Easter, or exchanging presents at Christmas, traditions can have deep meaning for us and our families. But they can sometimes prevent us from seeing how that holiday is truly meant to honor God. Take some time to reflect on the role traditions play in your worship:

List some traditions that you follow for holidays throughout the year.

- Tree & Ornaments
- Advent calendar
- Extra Christian stuff
- Hide eggs on Easter

How do these traditions bring you closer to God?

- Some of them remind us of God / reach us / help us grow in our faith

What are some ways they could turn your attention away from God if you're not intentional and careful?

- Go on autopilot
- Do so you don't feel guilt
- Value them over God

> Ask God to show you how common traditions might make it harder to follow Him and where those traditions might even contradict His commands to love Him and love your neighbor. Pray that you would always make following Him your priority in everything you do.

Spirit and Truth

Different Boxes

discover

READ MATTHEW 5:21-26.

*"So if you are offering your gift on the altar, and there you remember that your brother
or sister has something against you, leave your gift there in front of the altar. First go
and be reconciled with your brother or sister, and then come and offer your gift."*
—Matthew 5:23–24

Humans like to put things in categories, like boxes in our minds. For instance, adults talk about having a healthy "work/life" balance. Work activities go in one box and personal things go in another. This helps us remember to work hard but also to shift our attention and spend restful, quality time with our loved ones or our hobbies.

Unfortunately, we sometimes categorize our spiritual lives as well. For instance, we often think of our relationship with God in a different category than our relationships with other people. Worship goes in the "God" box and people go in the "regular life" box. But God sees the way we treat others as a reflection of our relationship with Him. That means the way we interact with other people is inseparable from our worship. So if we're having an argument with someone, Jesus actually says it's more important for us to go work that out before we worship God with our gifts and tithes. We can't put it in a separate box and worship God like nothing is wrong. For us to approach God with a heart that is prepared for sincere worship, we must first love our neighbors as Jesus commanded us.

delight

When in your life are you tempted to put off dealing with disagreements or arguments? Why would Jesus say you should deal with these before you worship?

- With my friends
- With outer family

Jesus says this so we can approach God prepared for sincere worship, without something in our hearts.

Jesus said the greatest commandment was to "love the Lord your God with all your heart and with all your soul and with all your mind" and to "love your neighbor as yourself" (Matt. 22:37-39). How does this relate to our key verses today (Matt. 5:23-24)?

Loving others is a way to show our love for God. We can also worship Him sincerely if we love our neighbor as ourself.

display

Is there a relationship you need to repair in your life? Maybe you need to apologize for hurtful words you said to your sibling or work out a disagreement between you and a friend. Work out some steps you can take to reconcile with that person and put that plan into action. Jesus calls us to live at peace with our neighbors and especially with our brothers and sisters in Christ.

Ask the Holy Spirit to guide you as you examine your heart. Are there any girls you regularly struggle to live at peace with? Take a minute to write out their names here. As you see these girls and feel your patience start to slip, pray "God, help me live at peace with ___Sadie___ (name) today."

- Sadie
- Bethany
- Audrey
- Isabelle
- Catharine
- Emerson
- Olive
- Francesca
- Ayla
- Gamma
- Genny
- Finley

- Grace
- Adelle
- Ella
- Grammy
- G-G Andy

Ask the Spirit to show you if there are any conflicts in your life that need to be addressed. If you are holding on to any anger, pray that your heart would be softened and that you would be able to humbly pursue reconciliation. Ask for divine help to guide your words and actions.

Knowing Jesus

discover |

READ JOHN 14:15-17.

"He is the Spirit of truth. The world is unable to receive him because it doesn't see him or know him. But you do know him, because he remains with you and will be in you. "
—*John 14:17*

In today's society, we are surrounded by conflicting messages in news reporting, social media, government officials, and advertisements. It can feel almost impossible to know what is true about anything. The internet is an incredible source of information, but it's too much information. It can be overwhelming, discouraging, and sometimes completely untrue.

That's why it's so important to know that as Christians, our ultimate source of truth is Jesus. He is true (see John 14:6), and the words He speaks are true (see John 1:14,17). He is the perfect, completely accurate image of God the Father (see Col. 1:15)—any quality we see in Jesus exists in His Father as well.

In today's passage, Jesus knew He would be leaving the disciples soon. He promised in His place He would send the Holy Spirit to be their counselor and their guide. That promise was not reserved for those disciples, though—all believers live with the Spirit as our guide, revealing Jesus and His ways to us. The Spirit allows us to go from just knowing facts about Jesus to actually knowing Jesus and His truth. Even when the world around us is confusing, we can be confident in knowing what is true about God through the work of the Spirit.

delight

What is the difference between knowing things about a person (such as a celebrity) and actually knowing a person (such as your best friend)?

Knowing about a person means knowing traits of them that they've revealed, but not knowing actually who them.

Knowing a person means having a relationship with that person and knowing personality traits they've revealed to you.

Would you say you know Jesus—that you have a relationship with Him? Or that you just know things about Jesus?

I do have a relationship with Jesus, but I feel like I don't know Him very well. I mostly know things about Him.

How can the Spirit help you grow your relationship with Jesus? How does the Spirit help you understand the truth of who Jesus is?

The Spirit can help me grow my relationship with Jesus by working in me. He can reveal who Jesus is by giving me understanding and by what He does inside me.

display

The Spirit also helps us see the truth of who God has made us to be. Through the Spirit, He has given each one of us unique gifts to grow His kingdom (see 1 Cor. 12:4-11; Rom. 12:6-8; 1 Pet. 4:10). Do you know what gifts God has given you? Ask your pastor, youth group leader, or parent if they can help you find a spiritual gifts assessment to take. You could also list areas that you know you are strong in (such as singing, art, organization, or humor).

What are some of your unique gifts, strengths, or talents?

- Academic Ability
- Empathy
- Sports

What are some ways you can use those gifts to grow God's kingdom?

I can spread the Word at academic competitions, show empathy and tell people about Jesus when doing that, and tell people about Jesus at my sporting events.

> **Praise God that when we don't know what is true, we can turn to the Spirit of truth in our midst. Ask for wisdom to respond with love and grace when the truth of a situation seems out of reach. Pray that the Spirit of truth would lead you to worship God with confidence that He is ultimately in control, no matter what.**

TRUTH

SECTION 3

To worship in truth means we must understand who God truly is and what He has done. If we worship without truth as our foundation, we might only worship those aspects of God we like—or worse, we might worship a god we have created in our image rather than the God who created us.

DAY 21

Long—Term Memory

discover |

READ JOHN 8:31-47.

"You will know the truth, and the truth will set you free."
—John 8:32

When Jesus told the crowd that knowing the truth would set them free, they were confused. Weren't they already free? They weren't in prison. They had never been slaves. They already had freedom! What's more, they were descended from Abraham and believed they were already guaranteed God's blessings (see Ps. 105:6; Isa. 41:8).

They had a selective memory about their history, though. Actually, God's people had been enslaved by many people in the past, like the Babylonians and the Egyptians. The people in the crowd may not have been slaves or prisoners, but their descendants certainly had. To that day, the Israelites were still dealing with the consequences of their sin. God allowed them to be conquered in the past so they would repent of their sin and return to Him.

Sin holds us captive because it separates us from God. Jesus said the only way to the Father was through Him (see John 14:6). When we choose to walk in the way of sin, we can't also follow Jesus (see 1 Cor. 10:21; Matt. 6:24). Jesus calls us to follow Him with all of our hearts. We have to pick one: follow Jesus and experience forgiveness of sin or follow the ways of sin and the world apart from God. There's no in-between. Following Jesus frees us from worshiping idols or lesser gods so that we can worship the Giver of life, our eternal source of hope.

delight

How have you seen the negative effects of sin in your life? How has it affected your worship?

Sin has held me back in my faith. It's given me guilt and even shame and has been a pin in my side always making me feel bad again. This is distracting and makes me feel discouraged and not want to worship.

In what ways has growing in your knowledge of Jesus and His truth changed your worship?

Growing in my knowledge of Jesus and His truth has changed how passionately I praise him, what I praise Him about, and has changed my perspective overall.

How has truth led to freedom in your life? Can you think of things that the truth of the gospel has freed you from?

Truth has led to the forgiveness of my sins and the gift of eternal life. The gospel's truth has freed me from idols (vanity, etc.), shame, and, most importantly, sin.

display

The Jews in the crowd had forgotten how God had saved His people over and over from the consequences of their sin and how much they needed to rely on Him. When we remember what God has done for us, we remember how trustworthy He is, and we can worship Him for faithfully providing for us even though we continue to sin. In the space below or in a notebook or prayer journal write about some of the ways God has been faithful in your life. How does His past provision for you inspire you to worship Him now?

- Mental Peace & Strength
- Happiness
- Fulfillment
- Letting go of shame
- Guidance and courage to stand out
- Love
- Purpose
- Courage
- Wisdom
- Strength
- He always answers our prayers
- He's given me what I need when I call out
- He never leaves us
- He never gives us too much to handle without providing an escape route

> **Praise God for the ways He has worked in your life in the past. Thank Him for sending Jesus to be the way, the truth, and the life, and pray that you would always be reminded of the truth of the gospel. Thank God that when the Son sets us free, we become truly and eternally free.**

Giving Back What Is His

discover

READ MARK 12:13-17.

Jesus told them, "Give to Caesar the things that are Caesar's, and to God the things that are God's." And they were utterly amazed at him.
—Mark 12:17

Like many of us today, the Jews in Jesus's time didn't like taxes. But they had an extra reason that most of us don't. Judea was under Roman occupation, so the Jews were paying taxes to the Roman government. Not only were they being ruled by a foreign government, but they had to pay them for it too.

The Pharisees, seeing an opportunity to trick Jesus, asked Him if it was correct for them to pay taxes to Rome. If Jesus answered *yes*, His followers might accuse Him of siding with the enemy. If he answered *no*, He could be arrested for treason against the emperor. Talk about a lose-lose situation!

Jesus once again answered in an unexpected way. Since the denarius He showed them was printed by Rome and bore Caesar's face, it was rightfully Caesar's to ask for. But in the same way, they should give God what was rightfully His. But what exactly is "God's"? How do we know what we're supposed to give Him? In the same way that coins were printed with the image of Caesar's face, every human being is created with the image of God imprinted on them (see Gen. 1:27). He has given us our very lives. So when we worship, we offer ourselves back to Him. We give Him our offerings, our service, and our praise because we know we are His.

delight |

What does it mean to be made in the image of God?

We were and are made by God and are His. We are similar to Him.

How does knowing you are God's and were made in His image affect the way you live?

Knowing this motivates me, makes me grateful, and changes my mindset.

What are some ways you give "to God the things that are God's"? What does this look like at school? At home? In your work or your activities? With your church?

At school, this could look like not gossiping, not conforming, spreading the Word, imaging Christ, etc. At home, this means helping out, being kind, talking about faith, and spending time with God (also in church).

display

Giving of our finances and our resources is one way we can give back to God out of what He has given us. Think about how you could do this. It could be in the form of tithes or financial gifts, volunteering with a local ministry, or any number of other things. List a few ways you could give back to Him and decide on one next step you could take this week. If you need ideas or need help getting started, talk to a parent, pastor, or other church leader.

Use an index card or create a lock-screen for your phone to display the words, "I am made in God's image. He has given me life, and I offer all that I am back to Him in worship." When you read these words, let them remind you that you are God's—always and no matter what—and He is worthy of all our worship.

- Tithe to church
  Donate
- Volunteer?
- Give to Chelsea,
      Mom, & Dad

If the subject of giving makes you uncomfortable, pray about this and ask God to help you search your heart. Thank Him for asking us to give freely out of love and gratitude, not demanding it from us. Praise Him for loving us and providing for us unconditionally and freely. Tell Him what you are grateful for today.

DAY 23

Truth in Worship

discover

READ JOHN 14:1-7.

Jesus told him, "I am the way, the truth, and the life. No one comes to the Father except through me."
—John 14:6

In 1938—years before televisions were common in American households—a breaking news story interrupted the normal programming on the Columbia Broadcasting Systems radio network: Martians had invaded New Jersey! This was, of course, not true—it was a radio play called *War of the Worlds* by the author Orson Welles. But many listeners didn't realize it was fictional, and their confusion caused a nationwide panic. At least, that's how the story goes. But now historians say that it might not be true. Newspapers at the time may have simply exaggerated the panic in an effort to discredit radio as a reliable source of news.[9]

So what's the truth? Was there really a panic or were newspapers to blame for spreading this false story of the gullible American public? We may never know for sure.

In the same way, we can be misled with false information about who Jesus is and what He taught. Not even every worship song represents Jesus accurately, and if we aren't careful, we can end up worshiping gods of our own making instead of the true God of the universe. Fortunately, we can trust Jesus's words about Himself to be true. Jesus Himself is the truth and an accurate image of God (see Col. 1:15), and we should avoid any worship that doesn't honor Jesus as He actually is.

delight

How can you know if you are really worshiping God as He truly is?

I can this by reading the Bible to inform myself, praying for directions, and talking to and watching other (especially more mature) Christians.
- And going to church, Bible study etc.

What are some misconceptions or lies about God you have been tempted to believe in the past? How did you come to believe the truth instead?

Some misconceptions about and lies about God I've been tempted to believe in the past include believing He is bad because bad things happen sometimes and believing in karma. I came to believe the truth through church + paying & reflecting over truth

Spirit and Truth

display

To know who God truly is, we need to be devoted to studying His Word regularly. One great way to do this is through individual Bible study. If you are not already studying the Bible on your own, choose a book you'd like to start reading. One of the Gospels is a great place to start. Read a short section every day, and as you go, write down any thoughts or questions you have. See if you can find the answers in Scripture itself. If you can't, ask a trusted spiritual mentor such as a pastor, youth leader, or parent to help you.

Thank God that the truth about Him isn't hidden—He has left us His Word and His Spirit to be our guides. Praise Him that we do not serve an unknowable, distant god but a God who loves us and wants to have a relationship with us. Pray that God would reveal Himself to you more and more through studying His Word, learning from teachers and pastors, and worshiping Him.

DAY 24

Weak Spots

discover

READ LUKE 18:9-14.

*"I tell you, this one went down to his house justified rather than
the other, because everyone who exalts himself will be humbled,
but the one who humbles himself will be exalted."*
—Luke 18:14

There are times in life when it's best to focus on our strengths, like when we're applying for a job. If you just list all your flaws in a job interview, you're most likely not going to get that job. The problem is, some people go through their whole lives like this, focusing only on the good in themselves. They may even think that they're kinder, wiser, smarter, or funnier than they really are—that they don't need to grow or improve because they're already perfect. It's hard to form a genuine relationship with someone who lacks humility like this. If they can't see the truth about themselves, how can they possibly be genuine with another person?

We can sometimes act this way with God too. Like the Pharisee here, we can think that we're living a good, God-honoring life and never look at the ways we're falling short. But let's face it: none of us worship God perfectly. As Paul wrote, "All have sinned and fall short of the glory of God" (Rom. 3:23). We all need His salvation because we aren't capable of saving ourselves. We can't have genuine worship if we can't face that truth. When we worship, we must do so with an attitude of humility, confessing to God that we need His mercy, forgiveness, and grace.

Spirit and Truth

delight

Have you ever thought like the Pharisee—being glad that you're "not as bad" as another person? What's wrong with this kind of attitude?

I have had this attitude. It's wrong because, with it, I can't thank God and worship Him genuinely.

How does humility and acknowledging the truth about ourselves help us worship more fully?

It helps us worship more fully because we can better understand and appreciate Jesus's sacrifice.

What truths about yourself might God be drawing your attention to?

There's something I've been holding onto that is keeping me from worshipping fully. I think it's my frustration,

display

David and the other psalmists used these poems and songs to express many emotions to God, including their humility, repentance, and sincere remorse for their sin. Take some time today to read one or two of the following psalms:

Psalm 25:1-11

Psalm 32

Psalm 51:1-12

Psalm 131

In the space below or in a journal, compare the psalmists' attitudes to those of the Pharisee and the tax collector in today's Scripture. How does this compare to your own attitude when you are disobedient and rebellious toward God?

Pharisee   T.C   Psalmids

Spend some time asking God to teach you humility. Ask Him to give you an accurate view of yourself—not so you can be ashamed of your flaws but so you can be honest with Him and with yourself. Ask for His forgiveness for your sin and ask Him to be gracious with you. Thank Him for loving you even when you believe you don't need Him.

MEMORY VERSE

Mark 12:29-31

Jesus answered,
"The most important is
Listen, Israel! The Lord our
God, the Lord is one.
Love the Lord your God
with all your heart, with
all your soul, with all your
mind, and with all your
strength. The second is,
Love your neighbor as
yourself. There is no
other command greater
than these."

Not Just a Story

discover |

READ JOHN 19:31-37.

*He who saw this has testified so that you also may believe. His
testimony is true, and he knows he is telling the truth.*
—John 19:35

This might seem like an odd passage to include in a book about worship.
You might be asking yourself, "What do dead men, broken legs, and a spear
piercing Jesus's side have to do with worshiping Him?" But this passage
is actually very important for our worship. With these words, the author
confirms that this isn't simply a story—he saw it himself as an eye-witness.

Worship can sometimes feel a bit removed from our day-to-day lives. We
have busy lives and the list of things to do can seem never ending. In all
this we're supposed to worship a God who we can't see and can't touch? It
would be so much easier if He would just speak with a great, booming voice
and tell us exactly what we want to know. Sometimes He feels distant. We
may wonder if He's even there.

When God starts to feel distant and unknowable, John's words can help
ground us in our faith. They remind us that when we read the Gospels, we
aren't simply reading stories about what God might be like—these aren't
legends or myths. The Gospels were written by people who lived alongside
Jesus and His apostles, who had up-close knowledge of Jesus and what He
was like. We can worship Jesus with confidence because of their faithful
accounts of His life, teachings, and works.

delight

When do you struggle most to worship? How can remembering the truth of who Jesus is help you at these times?

I struggle most to worship at school, TRC, Swim, Track, and late at night. Remembering the truth of who Jesus is will help because it will make me feel less distant and more inspired to glow with Him.

Why is it important for our worship to know we can trust the truth of the Gospels?

It is important because the Gospels tell us who Jesus is and what He did, which make up our worship and even shape our perspective about Him. Knowing the Gospels are the truth, we can worship with confidence.

display

When we read Scripture, we need to do more than just see words on a page. For God's Word to work in our hearts and in our lives, we need it to become part of us. In addition to reading His Word, listening to it can help. Give it a try! Find a recording of Scripture and choose a book of the Bible to start listening today. There are plenty of free recordings available. Check out the audio bibles at Bible Gateway (https://www.biblegateway.com/resources/audio/) or download an app. Bible Gateway, Streetlights, or YouVersion are great places to start.

Name a few Christian girls you know who'd like to grow in their faith too. Invite them to meet regularly (once a week, once a month, etc.) and read Scripture and talk about what you read together. As one girl reads aloud, follow along in your own Bible so you're hearing and seeing the words at the same time. Then dive back into the text to answer questions. The more you see and examine what's there, the more the Word becomes a part of your life.

Audrey
Isabelle
Bethany
Sadie

Ella
Catherine

Pray that even in your busy life, God would remind you that He is the ultimate source of truth and goodness. Thank Him that we can trust what we know about Him because He sent His Son to be our teacher and our salvation, once and for all. Thank Him for the Bible and its trustworthy accounts of who He is and what He is like.

DAY 26

From the Heart

discover |

READ MATTHEW 6:5-8.

Don't be like them, because your Father knows the things you need before you ask him.
—Matthew 6:8

When we pray, we might think we need to use impressive words. Especially if we're asked to pray aloud, we may think our prayers need to "sound good." We may listen to other people and think, "I could never pray like that! They sound like they know what they're talking about, and I just stumble over my words."

The truth is, God just wants to hear from us. Prayer isn't a performance, and it's not about sounding good. It's about having a conversation with our almighty Father. In these verses, Jesus said hypocrites pray with lots of fancy-sounding words they don't actually believe so people will hear them and think they're holy and righteous. That's why He says to pray in private—not because our prayers need to be secret but because then we won't be tempted to show off when we pray. When we pray in private, our prayers can be a conversation just between us and God without worrying about the words we use. He knows what's in our hearts; He just wants us to bring it to Him in whatever way we can.

This doesn't mean praying aloud in front of others is bad, of course. But even when we pray aloud, we shouldn't make it into a performance or be untrue with our words. Our prayers should come from our hearts and we should mean every word we speak.

delight

How does it feel when you pray by yourself versus praying aloud around other people?

When I pray by myself I sometimes overthink things and it's too hard to understand anything. Praying with others holds me steady and accountable, but I am tempted to show off.

How can you practice praying from your heart no matter the circumstances? How does this honor God?

I can practice praying from my heart by trying to focus only on Jesus in my circumstance. This honors God because we are being genuine, humble, and honest, and are pursuing Him.

How can you remind yourself that prayer isn't about impressing God but growing closer to Him?

I can remind myself that prayer isn't about impressing God by remembering what prayer is, what it's purpose is, and what God expects of me. This will hold me accountable and remind me to be grateful of the wonderful gift of prayer and that God always answers them.

display

Journaling your prayers is a great way to have a meaningful conversation with God without the need for fancy words. When you pray in a journal, you can write whatever comes to mind. You don't even need to write in complete sentences—no one needs to see it but you and God! You can even draw or doodle, use multiple colors, write upside down or sideways, write in ALL CAPS if you're angry or excited, write lists . . . the sky's the limit! Today, open up a notebook and try journaling your prayers or write a response to the prompt below.

Dear God, today I'd like to talk to You about . . .

my daily struggles
- I overthink how high my terrors are
- I ruin Your name into blasphemy
- I worry about corrupting myself
- I worry about failure and its consequences
- I worry about evil
- I worry about being grateful
- I worry about causing someone to go to hell
- I worry about conforming

In a journal or in whatever form of prayer feels most comfortable for you, thank God that He doesn't require us to use certain words or language when we pray. Tell Him about the times you felt your prayers were inadequate. Use this time to practice praying truthfully and from your heart, not worrying about how your prayers sound to God or whether they would sound impressive to anyone else.

Spirit and Truth

A Heavy Burden

discover |

READ JOHN 16:12-15.

When the Spirit of truth comes, he will guide you into all the truth. For he will not speak on his own, but he will speak whatever he hears. He will also declare to you what is to come.
—John 16:13

You don't need to have seen the film *A Few Good Men* to have heard one of its most memorable lines: Jack Nicholson emphatically shouting, "You can't handle the truth!" Truth can be a heavy thing. There's a reason we don't teach children some of the heavier truths of life until they're a bit older. They need to mature a bit first.

Likewise, Jesus knew His disciples were still maturing spiritually. He had already given them a lot to think about, and they hadn't even fully understood that. The Father had given Jesus a heavy burden to bear, and the disciples weren't strong enough yet to share that burden with Him. Instead, He told them that later, the Spirit would come and teach them the things Jesus could not share with them quite yet. The Spirit would guide them to it and help them to bear it.

This same Spirit helps us now know, understand, and bear the hard truths of following Jesus. Let's face it: worshiping Christ with our service and obedience is not always easy. It requires sacrifice, courage, and perseverance. However, if we claim Jesus as our Lord, we can trust that the Spirit will work in us to make that truth beautiful and life-giving, even when it's hard.

delight

What have been some times in your life that the truth—either about Jesus or something else—seemed too much to bear? How did God help you bear that truth?

~ King of kings - Gave me peace.
- Non-Christians will go to hell
- I will exist forever
- My life isn't under my control
- All are equal
- Hard things will happen
- Gave me peace & understanding
that He will be with me,
is for me, that all are
equal under God, that
His plans - perfect and that
I will live in paradise

How has the Spirit helped you understand truths about Jesus and the gospel that seemed difficult at first? How has this changed the way you worship?

- Showed me His holiness
- Showed me His forgiveness
mercy, patience, & love
- Showed me His power
- More grateful (sm things too
desperate)
- In awe
- Reverence

display

When we have difficult things to face, we often try to do it on our own. But God calls believers to share our burdens with one another (see Gal. 6:2). This week find one way you can serve your church community or a Christian girl who's in need. Talk with a leader or parent if you need help coming up with ideas. Alternately, if you feel like you're struggling yourself, what are some ways you can ask for help from your family, friends, or community?

Think about the girls around you who are following Jesus too. Next time you hang out, talk about some ways you could serve other Christians together.

Talk to God about some of the more difficult truths that come along with being a follower of Jesus. Ask the Spirit to give you strength and comfort when you are struggling. Pray that when life feels heavy, you could turn your frustration or sorrow into praise for the God who never leaves us alone and who never forgets us in our troubles.

Dos and Don'ts

discover

READ MARK 12:28-34.

Jesus answered, "The most important is Listen, Israel! The Lord our God, the Lord is one. Love the Lord your God with all your heart, with all your soul, with all your mind, and with all your strength."
—Mark 12:29-30

When we're children, we discover that life is full of rules. "Look both ways before crossing the street." "Don't yell in the house." "Share your toys." In most cases the rules we learned were there to help teach us or keep us safe. But sometimes we end up thinking that all of life works that way: When you follow the rules, good things happen. When you break the rules, there are consequences.

Relationships aren't based on rules, however. The rules are just a starting place to teach us how to live. In the end what really matters are qualities such as kindness, generosity, love, and respect. Focusing on "dos and don'ts" makes our relationships more complicated than they need to be—and probably less authentic too.

God didn't give us commands to regulate our relationship with Him, either. His commands teach us how to live in His ways and how much we need Him to help us. Ultimately, our relationship with Him should be based in love. When we worship Him in Spirit and truth, with our whole hearts, minds, souls, and strength—when we give Him the best of who we are—our love for Him will grow deeper with each passing day, and we will be able to rejoice in the blessings that a relationship with Him brings.

delight

What are some ways you might be treating your faith like a series of rules?

What would it look like to center your faith on a loving relationship with God instead?

How can worship be a way to practice loving God "with all your heart, with all your soul, with all your mind, and with all your strength" (v. 30)?

display

Some of the most beautiful art in history was created as an act of worship. Michelangelo's paintings in the Sistine Chapel, Handel's Messiah, and Christ the Redeemer in Rio de Janeiro were all created to celebrate our amazing God. We don't need to be world-renowned artists to honor our God through art. Take some time today to use art or crafts as a form of worship. This could be through any medium: drawing, painting, photography, doodling, knitting, writing, baking, sculpture, collage, or even just spending some quiet time coloring. Let the Spirit show you how to experience God's truth through creativity. Even if you are not an artistic person, give this a try. No matter your skill level, whatever you do, focus your heart and mind on God as you create and He will be glorified!

Thank God that worshiping Him isn't about following rules and that what He wants more than anything is for us to love Him. Ask Him to show you how you can love Him best today. Also ask Him to show you any ways that you are focusing too much on trying to earn His approval through following rules or your works.

Love One Another

discover |

READ MARK 12:28-34; MATTHEW 5:43-48.

"The second is, Love your neighbor as yourself. There is no other command greater than these."
—Mark 12:31

"By this everyone will know that you are my disciples, if you love one another" (John 13:35). Jesus shared these words with His disciples the night before He was betrayed and crucified. Loving people who love us back is easy. Jesus calls us to do more than that—He calls us to include our enemies in the circle of that love. Jesus calls us to radically change the way we interact with everyone around us.

Fortunately, Jesus doesn't expect us to do this out of our own power. We can love others because Jesus loved us first. His love and His Spirit empower us to love even the most seemingly unlovable people—those who have humiliated us, betrayed us, or even people who hate us. We are called to forgive and extend kindness to all people.

Loving our neighbors as ourselves means all our neighbors, not just the ones we like. And it means more than simply tolerating difficult people—Jesus calls us to the difficult task of actually loving them as we love ourselves. Following this command is a profound act of worship—it shows that we trust His commands to be true. They may not be easy for us, but we trust that they are for our good and for the good of His kingdom.

delight

Think of a girl you would consider an enemy or a girl you find difficult to like. What would it look like to love her this week?

What is one shift in your thinking that would help you see her in a different light? How does it help to remember that God loves her?

display

Jesus said the greatest commands were to love God and love our neighbors. Therefore, the greatest worship we can give God must align with these two commands. Loving our neighbor isn't always easy, but it's essential if we call ourselves followers of Christ. Brainstorm some ways you can love a girl who is a neighbor to you: a classmate, a family member, a church member, or a physical neighbor on your street or block. Put one of these ideas into practice today.

These are some ways I can love a neighbor today:

Thank God for His upside-down kingdom where He calls us to reverse the attitudes and actions that are so natural to us—loving our enemies instead of hating them; enduring suffering instead of avoiding it; praying for those who persecute us instead of cursing them. Confess to Him how these commands are sometimes difficult for you to follow, and pray that He would give you the strength and compassion to love others the way He loves you.

Seek God First

discover

READ MATTHEW 6:25-34.

*"But seek first the kingdom of God and his righteousness, and
all these things will be provided for you."*
—Matthew 6:33

How often is God at the front of your mind? Most of us would have to admit, "Sometimes, but not always." When life gets busy and we're juggling responsibilities and activities, we often end up just fitting Him in wherever we can—if we remember to at all. For many people, the only time they even think about God is on Sunday mornings or when things fall apart and they don't know where else to turn. Going to God becomes our last resort instead of our first priority.

Jesus tells us that our priorities are in the exact wrong order. We spend our time being anxious about food, clothing, money, work, grades, and whatever else we think we need, but we don't need to worry! God knows what we need and it is His delight to provide it to us. If we simply turn to Him first, we can rest assured knowing He has everything under control. When we focus on Him before anything else, all the rest will fall into place.

When we live a lifestyle of worshiping God with all that we are—in the truth of who He is and through the power of His Spirit—we allow His power and presence to work in us. We will see His works and feel His presence more and more in our lives. We will shine with His light wherever we go, displaying it for everyone around us to see.

delight

What are some things you tend to worry about? How can you give those things to God and trust that He will provide what you need?

What have you learned about worship in the past thirty days that has changed your relationship with God? How can you carry these lessons forward in your life and walk with Jesus?

display

What are you most worried about right now? What are you striving toward or hoping for? When we find ourselves swept away by anxiety instead of being consumed by our worry, believers have access to a better solution. We put everything into God's hands and trust that the story He is writing for our life is better than anything we can imagine. Today, write down some of the things that are occupying your thoughts lately. Look back through the devotions from the past thirty days and list some ways worship can help you turn your attention away from your worries and back onto Him.

As we close our thirty days of devotions on worship, pray that the Spirit would work through what you have learned and that He would use it to draw you ever closer to the God who is worthy of all of our worship and praise. Thank God for any insights He has given you through this time focusing on Him.

R-E-V-E-R-E-N-C-E

Reverence is a somewhat vague and churchy word, but rather than brushing it aside as one of those words we just hear in church, let's break it down.

R: RESPECT

To respect someone means we see them as having great value, give them our attention and affection, and consider who they are when we speak to or interact with them.

Name one way you can show God respect.

Don't use His name in vain
Obey Him
Thank Him

How has God shown you respect?

He is infinitely patient

E: EXPECTATION

God expects us to obey, though He understands we will not obey perfectly. We can also expect Him to be who He says He is—the one true God who is very much worthy of our honor and praise.

Describe a time when God showed up—when you saw evidence in your own life that God is exactly who He says He is.

I was having a hard time with intrusive thoughts and putting my trust in God. When I allowed Him control, unexplainable ...

What's one step of obedience God might be calling you to take today?

To stop trying to be cool when I know it will cause me to sin. But to not judge.

V: VALUE

We value God when we show Him the respect and honor He deserves as the Holy and righteous God and our loving, compassionate Father. When we show God reverence, we're saying He is worthy of our time, attention, and affection.

How much time do you spend with God on a typical day? What does this say about your value of God versus the value you place on other things?

In what ways has God shown you that you are valuable to Him?

E: EXPRESSION

Reverence toward God isn't just something for us to hold inside. We are called to express our reverence through our prayers, our praise, and our daily thoughts, words, and actions. In all that we do, we should consider who God is and what our purpose is.

How did Jesus teach us to show reverence to God in the way He lived, talked, and prayed?

What are some ways you can express your reverence to God individually and with other Christians?

R: REVELATION

God has revealed Himself to us through Jesus and His Word, the Bible. He does not hide who He is from us but makes Himself present and known in our lives through the Holy Spirit. We can know God and all the many ways He's worthy of our awe and respect.

Spirit and Truth

What has God revealed to you about Himself as you study the Bible?

God is actively working, even if I can't always see or feel it.

How can you point others to the ways God has revealed Himself to us?

By living with love and according to His commandments.

E: ETERNAL

God is eternal—He has always existed and always will. Part of our purpose—to glorify God—isn't just for the here and now; we were made to worship Him forever (see Rev. 5:11-13). Though our worship will be different when we see Him face to face, He will still be the God who is worthy of our honor and praise.

How does it affect you to know the relationship God invites you into isn't just for the here and now?

- I feel better about suffering

We can read about what heaven might be like in Revelation, but we won't truly know until we're there. What do you imagine worship will be like in heaven?

N: NOBILITY

3/1-12Art - gave him a lot to He, Praise be!

God isn't only the Creator of all, He's the Ruler of all too. When we approach God, it's good to remember that we're approaching a holy and righteous King who stands above all other rulers past or present. He is excellent in every way.

God asks for our loyalty (see Ex. 20:2). What things or people have you put before them? How can you return them to their rightful place?

I've put makeup, popularity, pleasing my friends, and being a good swimmer before them. I can return them by remembering my purpose and remembering.

What are some ways God has shown you that He is a good, kind, and compassionate King?

He always gives me peace when I need it. He helps me and talent worth when I give situations to Him, which doesn't Creation I always should things always work out right. His worth Plans are perfect